20 Men's Jobs of the 1800s

The Works That Forged a Nation

Preface

Certainly, any attempt in such a small volume to present and describe the histories of even just twenty men's jobs in the American 1800s falls far short. This book can only hope to stimulate interest and further research into these occupations. Opportunities to dive into your own personal interests by way of the internet and public libraries are limitless. Hopefully, this brief glimpse at these occupations will motivate you to do so.

The twenty jobs touched upon here obviously cover only a tiny number of the innumerable day-to-day tasks of Americans well over a century ago. There was a great deal of overlap among these jobs, nor they were done only by adult males. Many would have required the diligent, persistent labor and cooperation of the entire extended family and neighbors.

In 1831, French diplomat and historian Alexis de Tocqueville toured the United States for nine months. In 1835 he published the first volume "*Democracy in America*." He noted that America's spirit of individualism and freedom of thought resulted in a practical application of scientific knowledge. *"The Americans,"* he wrote, *"always display a clear, free, original and inventive power of mind."*

The major influence that drove America's technological development was the expansion of the nation's boundaries, population, and economy. The territorial size of the United States quadrupled from 1800 to 1900 as it spanned the continent. The population grew from 5.3 million people in 1800 to 75 million in 1900.

The most influential technology of the 19th century was steam power, providing a more consistent source of power than water or wind.

The 19th century was also a time of genius inventors. Samuel Morse's invention of the telegraph (1835) and Alexander Graham Bell's telephone (1876) made long-distance communication possible. In 1846, Elias Howe patented the sewing machine. In his lifetime, Thomas A. Edison amassed more than 1,300 patents.

Wiley Bryant Henderson

Chapel Hill, North Carolina, USA

April 2022

20 The Wheelwright

AGRICULTURE and FOOD

1. The Farmer

In early America, agriculture was the primary livelihood for 90% of the people. Many towns and cities sprang up as shipping points for the export of agricultural products. Natural waterways and manmade canals were affordable means of shipping. After the 1830s railroads became played a major role in westward expansion.

Yearly each farmer raised enough food for three to five people. Revolutionary developments took place during the 1800s that boosted the production of the American farming family.

Where the farmer lived determined the specific crops that he grew. Most would grow wheat, barley, oats, rice, corn, vegetables, and more. In the Southern states, cotton, tobacco, rice, and "naval stores" – tar, pitch, and turpentine from the longleaf pine forests – were highly profitable.

Many types of livestock were tended, such as beef and dairy cattle, hogs, chickens, ducks, geese, and more. Eggs and feathers from the fowl and dairy products like butter and cheese were valuable food sources for the farm family. They also were valuable to sell and/or trade.

After 1800, cotton became the chief crop in southern plantations, and the most valuable American export. Eli Whitney's invention of the cotton gin in 1794 improved the profitability of cotton farming. Connecting a gin to water or steam power hugely boosted the capacity to process greater amounts of cotton fiber.

Westward expansion, including the Louisiana Purchase and American victory in the War of 1812, plus the building of canals and the introduction of steamboats opened new areas for agriculture.

■ ■

2. The Plowman

The job of the plowman (ploughman) was to plow the land, with a plow pulled by horses or oxen. Because plows and draft animals were expensive, many farmers would hire the plowman to prepare their fields. The plowman would often provide his own plow and animals.

Plowing was a seasonal job; it was common for a community to own the plow itself, and to have its own plowman. His function was to plow for all the independent farms in the area. They, in turn, would provide for his income. He would often then hire out as a farm worker for the rest of the year.

Plowing a field was a hard and time-consuming task. It called for physical strength in handling the plow and the draft animals, attention to detail, and perseverance. Skillful plowing turns and aerates the soil, controls weeds, improves drainage, improves the soil structure, and reduces the risk of disease.

John Deere had invented a steel plow capable of slicing through tough sod in 1838; James Oliver improved it in 1868. Wheat production doubled from 1860 to 1890.

Since the mid 1800's, there has been enormous change in plow development. Horse plows soon became outdated; more efficient steam tractors worked with large multi-furrow balance plows.

✱✱
✱✱✱

3. The Orchardman

In the 19th century, apples came in all shapes and types. Some were as misshapen as potatoes, others with rough, sandpapery skin. They ranged in size from a cherry to a grapefruit. In America in the 19th century there were around 14,000 varieties grown.

In the early days of America, because of diseases such as typhoid fever and cholera, people did not drink water very often. Instead, hard cider was the drink of choice — even children drank it.

The apples that John Chapman "Johnny Appleseed" brought to the frontier were completely different from the apples available at today's grocery store or farmers' market. They weren't mainly for eating. They were used to make America's beverage-of-choice at the time, hard apple cider.

Apple cider gave those on the frontier a safe, stable source of drink. Cider was drunk in a time when water could be dangerous. Transplanted New

Englanders on the frontier drank a reported 10.52 ounces of hard cider per day (the average American today drinks 20 ounces of water a day).

During the Civil War, women took control of the farms and businesses as the menfolk went off to fight; many aided in a war effort for the first time in American history. When the men returned home, expected their wives to go back to their old roles and give up their independence. Women began to organize for their civil and political rights as never before.

4. The Fisherman

Today, many think of fishing as putting bait on a hook, dropping it in the water, and hoping a fish swims by and takes the bait. Such fishing was common in 19th century America, but more efficient methods were also used.

Each year during April and May most American rivers would be filled with shad and herring spawning upriver. During fishing season, everyone except the cook and the housekeeper were netting and processing the fish "24/7." Because there is such a narrow window of opportunity, the activity was non-stop.

One important means of reaping a huge harvest of fish was known as "pulling the seine.". One end of the big net to a tree or to a "dead man's post" brace. Boats would launch into the water, make a semicircle, come back to shore, and hand off the net and the hauling line. A group onshore would pull on the line, cinching up the bottom of the net. The group waded into the water with bushel baskets, tossing the fish onshore.

The heads were removed, and the fish gutted. These discarded items would be used as fertilizer. The body cavities were packed with salt. The dressed fished were often placed into barrels for storage or shipment. Properly preserved fish could last well over a year.

A fishing weir is an obstruction placed in tidal waters, or wholly or partially across a river, to direct the passage of, or trap fish. A weir may be used to trap marine fish in the intertidal zone as the tide recedes, fish such as salmon or eels. Weirs were traditionally built from wood or stones. The earliest steam powered fishing boats first appeared in the 1870s and used the trawl system of fishing as well as lines and drift nets.

5. The Net Maker

Net making has been a craft for thousands of years for a wide range of uses, from sports to the haulage of loads and protecting crops from birds. It's generally accepted that the earliest nets were used for fishing. Early nets were woven from grasses, flaxes and other fibrous plant material. Later cotton was used.

First Net

The first known net, known as the net of Antrea, dates from 8300BC. Along with other fishing equipment, it was unearthed in the town of Antrea - which became known as Kamennogorsk in 1946 - in Russia.

Made from willow, it was discovered by farmer Antti Virolainen in 1913 in a swamp that had been the Ancylus Lake. It measured 27 to 30m long and 1.3 to 1.5m wide, with a mesh of 6cm. It was suspected that a fishing boat had capsized, causing the loss of the net and all the equipment.

Many examples of fishing nets have been documented in ancient Greek literature and Egyptian tomb paintings, while Roman mosaics have also featured nets.

Manufacturing Net

Evidence from *The Domesday Book* reveals that twine and nets were being manufactured on a large scale in England as long ago as the 11th century. Net making was a cottage industry for many people, with outworkers toiling from home.

It was often women's work, completed in between their other tasks such as cooking, tending the cattle or laboring in the fields. Children were also enlisted to help and net making was a skill taught early to every family member.

Net was made using twine, a block of wood called a lace and a wooden needle. The needle was threaded with twine and gripped in one hand, while the lace was held in the other hand. The twine was stretched across to the lace and secured with a braider's knot. This continued until the net took shape - it could be made to any size. In the 19th century, mills that made net provided employment for thousands of people.

Bird Netting

Bird netting is a form of cruelty-free pest control, used globally to stop birds from eating and pecking at crops.

In 18th and 19th century England, netting was used to keep birds off home-grown crops, particularly in walled gardens such as the one described in Frances Hodgson Burnett's novel, *The Secret Garden*.

The eight-acre walled garden at historic Brocklesby Park estate in Lincolnshire was built by English landscape architect, Lancelot 'Capability' Brown, in the 18th century. Queen Victoria had a 31-acre kitchen garden built in 1844, employing 150 gardeners. According to landscape architect, award-winning gardener and writer Bunny Guinness, such gardens were vital to feed the huge households of the day. They ensured that the privileged few had treats, such as all-year-round fresh fruit or asparagus at Christmas.

The height of productivity for these walled gardens was between around 1800 and 1940. Guinness describes how simple hot walls, as well as greenhouses, helped to mature the fruit. Copings often overhung the wall by around 15cm, so for extra protection, metal brackets that protruded by around 60cm were fitted to the fruit walls, so that nets could be hung vertically - nurturing and protecting the fruit.

'Hot beds' were protected by nets and covered by large amounts of manure to promote the growth of early salad vegetables and even melons.

Another popular method of deterring birds from crops, particularly in 19th century England, was the fruit cage. Queen Victoria's fruit and vegetable garden at Osborne House had a selection of beautifully ornate cages, in addition to bird netting.

Today's professional anti-bird netting comes in large rolls - a cost-effective option for farmers and agricultural businesses who require bulk quantities. Smaller packages are available for the amateur gardener. Equally applicable for vineyard bird control and to bird proof buildings against urban bird species such as gulls and pigeons, bird netting helps to manage bird activity, noise, and mess.

6. The Sail Maker

Making sails required considerable skill. To function well, a sail needs to be both strong enough to withstand the power of the wind, but also to be light and flexible enough to be handled by sailors working aloft, often in very challenging conditions.

It was discovered many centuries ago, that if a seafarer were to take a flattened piece of animal skin or some type of woven mat and attach it to a couple of tree limbs, secure it to his boat and wait for a breeze to blow, the paddles could be set to the side while the power of the wind propelled the vessel across the water.

During the early years, it would require acres of canvas, long and laborious hours of hand-stitching and painstaking precision in cutting skills to produce even one sail.

A sailmaker makes and repairs sails for sailboats, kites, hang gliders, wind art, architectural sails, or other structures using sails. A sailmaker typically works on shore in a sail loft; the sail loft has other sailmakers. Large ocean-going sailing ships often had sailmakers in the crew.

7. The Miller

A miller is a person who operates a mill, a machine to grind a grain (for example corn or wheat) to make flour. Milling is among the oldest of human occupations. The materials ground by millers are often foodstuffs and particularly grain.

Although the terms "gristmill" or "corn mill" can refer to any mill that grinds grain, the terms were used historically for

Farmers brought their own grain to a local mill and received ground meal or flour. Early mills were almost always built and supported by farming communities and the miller received the "miller's toll" in lieu of cash. Most towns and villages had their own mill so that local farmers could easily transport their grain there to be milled

Mills in the 1800s were usually water-powered, though some were driven by the wind or by livestock. In most watermills the water wheel was mounted vertically. Later designs incorporated horizontal steel or cast iron turbines and these were sometimes refitted into the old wheel mills.

Early sawmills simply adapted the whipsaw to mechanical power, generally driven by a water wheel to speed up the process. Later, the circular motion of the wheel was changed to back-and-forth motion of the saw blade.

COMMUNICATIONS

8. The Printer

During the nineteenth century the productivity of presses increased greatly, partly because of improvements in their construction and partly because of the use of steam to power them. As a result, print becomes more affordable and accessible to the working class.

American printers printed books, newspapers, pamphlets, and other publications. Their shops sometimes served as mail centers Paper was made from linen and cloth and ink was made from tannin, iron sulfate, gum, and water.

Printing a publication such a newspaper was a complicated task. First, the type was set. A type was a single piece of metal with a letter, number, or point of punctuation. Setting the type was a slow, cumbersome job. A single page of a colonial newspaper could take up to 25 hours of labor to produce.

9. The Mail Man

On July 26, 1775, the **U.S. postal system** is established by the Second Continental Congress, with Benjamin Franklin as its first postmaster general. **Paper envelopes** had been developed in China, where paper was invented in the 2nd century BCE.

Stagecoaches

By the late 1700s, **stagecoaches** (large horse-drawn vehicles) had begun to replace individual **post riders** on the roads. At the urging of Congress, the post office granted contracts to stagecoach lines to help link Eastern communities with the expanding frontier.

Steamboats

Congress authorized the postmaster general to contract with steamboat companies to move the mail in 1813, six years after Robert Fulton launched the first successful commercial steamboat line in New York. By the late 1820s, steamboats were ferrying mail up and down the East Coast and along the Mississippi River.

Pony Express

Those looking for a speedier delivery could, for a short time, at least, turn to the **Pony Express**, a private service that began running between St. Joseph, Missouri, 0and California in April 1860. The post office contracted with the Pony Express for only a few months before the service shut down in October 1861, shortly after the completion of the transcontinental telegraph line.

Railroads

Though the post office first transported mail via the "iron horse" in 1832, its use of the railroad entered a new era of efficiency after the Civil War, with the completion of the nation's first transcontinental railroad. From the 1860s to the 1970s, clerks would sort and distribute mail on trains crossing the country.

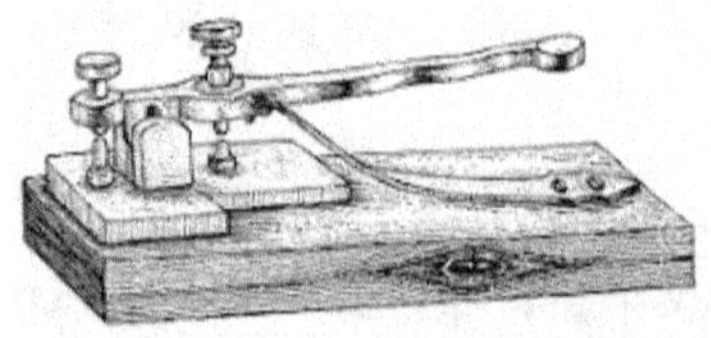

10. The Telegrapher

A telegrapher is an operator who uses a telegraph key to send and receive the Morse code to broadcast electrical signals over a wire strung between stations.

In 1844, Samuel F.B. Morse sent the first telegraph message from Baltimore to Washington, reading, *What hath God wrought?*

Morse (1791-1872) and other inventors developed, the telegraph in the 1830s and 1840s. It revolutionized long-distance communication forever.

The job of the telegrapher was to transfer information between the train dispatcher and the train operator. A telegrapher copied train orders and messages from the train crew and reported the passing trains to the dispatcher.

During the Civil War the new technology of the telegraph was a hugely important factor of the victory of Union forces. Processing over 6.5 million messages during the war, the *United States Military Telegraph Service* (USMT) built 15,000 miles of line. In contrast the South used the telegraph in only the most limited fashion.

For the first time in the history of warfare, the telegraph helped field commanders during the Civil War to direct real-time battlefield operations and permitted senior military officials to coordinate strategy across large distances. These abilities were key factors in the North's victory.

Ulysses S. Grant wrote that he had *held frequent conversations over the wires* about strategy with US Secretary of War Stanton during 1863. Stanton depended on the telegraph to check the actions of generals in the field, and President Lincoln spent long hours in the War Department telegraph office.

CONSTRUCTION

Ramp-loaded brickmaking machine by Henry Clayton, c. 1840.

11. The Brickmaker

Brickmakers were important in towns, and their trade contributed to the overall appearance of the village or city. Brickmakers made their products by digging clay from the ground.

The mixture would then be placed in a wooden mold to make the right shape. Within the molds, the brick mixtures would dry for a week, then moved to a drying shed for storage up to six weeks.

The excellent quality and abundance of local clays in the states made it unnecessary to import bricks from across the Atlantic. Brick-making centers developed along the rivers and the Atlantic coast.

The main ingredients were clay and sand or shale. Next, the clay was screened to remove rocks and the shale and clay were ground into powder by a crusher and stored.

In the Pug Mill, water was added to the powder and the clay and sand mixture was soaked, stirred, and kneaded with large augers or wooden paddles until doughy. This step was called tempering or pugging.

Before the invention of steam-driven machines, bricks were molded by hand. The real break-through came in 1852, when a steam-powered machine was developed by Richard VerValen.

Dryer sheds were located within the factory. These "green bricks" were dried for 3 days.

The dried bricks were arranged into arches and the fire built inside the arch -- the bricks themselves were the kiln. The kilns were originally fired with wood. When the bricks were sufficiently fired, the heat was reduced, and they were allowed to cool gradually before removal from the kiln.

12. The Carpenter

Carpentry is a skilled trade and a craft in which the primary work performed is the cutting, shaping and installation of building materials during the construction of buildings, ships, timber bridges, concrete formwork, etc. Historically, building methods were passed down from a master carpenter to an apprentice verbally, through demonstration, and through work experience.

Carpentry is one of the traditional trades but is not always clearly distinguished from the work of the joiner and cabinetmaker, in general, a carpenter historically did the heavier, rougher work of framing a building. In short, a carpenter builds buildings.

Before the mid-nineteenth century in America, most carpenters worked under the artisan system. After a four-to seven-year stint as an apprentice the carpenter became a journeyman. The Journeyman carpenter during this time worked indoors and outdoors.

During the 1840s, 18505, and 1860s, planing mills and door, sash, and blind factories took over the indoor work once done by journeymen. Semi-skilled workers operated machines that mass-produced the doors, moldings, and window frames that journeymen carpenters once crafted by hand.

13. The Cooper

Coopers were tradesman who made casks, buckets, barrels, and containers for flour, gunpowder, tobacco, shipping, wine, milk, and other liquids. Every year, American coopers made millions of such containers.

Cooperage in the 19th century was learned through an apprenticeship system. This one-to-one instruction was necessary to ensure that apprentices mastered the skills necessary to produce barrels that would hold valuable contents.

In making a barrel, a cooper first shaped the staves, which are the individual pieces that run from the top to the bottom of the barrel. The staves were split (riven) or sawn using draw knives and a jointer plane. The cooper relied on an experienced eye to taper the staves at the ends, which were left wide in the middle to create the center bulge of the barrel.

The fishing industry used barrels for shipping pickled and dried fish. Farmers used them for storing grains, butter, and cider. Merchants used them for storing hardware and dried goods. The whaling industry used barrels to store tools and provisions, and of course whale oil.

White oak was used for casks that held liquids. Red oak, ash, chestnut, pine, and spruce were used for dried goods and everything in between – salted meat, butter, oils, paint, white lead, and even dangerous chemicals like arsenic.

14. The Mason - Brick and Stone

Beginning in the 1800s. brick became a popular building material in major U.S. cities because they are more fire-resistant than wood.

It is interesting to note that the terms "mason and "bricklayer" are titles which are used interchangeably by the public. There is a difference in skillset. Bricklayers are typically focused on building with clay or concrete bricks, and blocks.

Masons focus on construction involving stone, marble, granite, and other similar natural materials. Grand castles constructed using localized stone can be found throughout England, Ireland, Scotland, France, and Germany.

Such techniques as erecting stone fences with no mortar can be found throughout North America where stonemasons hand-cut and fitted stones in a stable fashion. Such walls stand strong to this day.

Apprenticeship for becoming a bricklayer took three to four years, with three years of schooling and several thousand hours of apprenticeship work combined. Qualified bricklayers could move on to become stonemasons as much of the skill sets are interchangeable.

15. The Saddle Maker

Saddle making is one of the few trades that hasn't changed much through the years. Other than some very minor use of power tools, most saddles are made the same today as they were in the 1800s. Just as people are all different, so are horses. Skilled Each saddle is made by hand, custom fitting each to fit the horse and meet the needs of the rider.

A saddle that fits one horse well won't necessarily fit another. Saddle makers would have several different styles of "trees," each of which is available in different sizes. A poorly made saddle could cause irritation and even injury to a valuable horse.

While saddle making and harness making were different trades, there would usually only be one saddle or harness maker in a town – if there even was one. This meant that the saddle maker could easily find himself doing repairs and adjustments to all sorts of leather goods.

A common task was making harnesses for draft horses. Making harness is mostly just a series of straps sewn together or attached with buckles and other fittings. Still, most often, only the saddle maker had the necessary tools for this work. A harness could cost a month's wages, take thirty hours to make, and would last 25-30 years.

The job of a harness or saddle maker was hard work. Apprenticeships usually started around age 13, and apprentices had to learn the complexities of fashioning systems of cutting, stitching, and assembly that connected a horse to a carriage.

16. The Cobbler

Shoemakers made shoes first by making wooden "lasts," or blocks of foot-shaped wood carved into different sizes. Next, a leather "upper" was stretched over the last and fastened with glue until it was ready to be fastened to the sole. The sole would be pounded with metal tools and an awl was used to cut holes.

Then the upper was removed from the last and sole and upper were sewn together the shoes and fitted with heels. A standard pair of shoes would take between eight and ten hours to make. As late as the 1850s, shoemakers used the same pattern to make a pair of shoes, meaning the left and right shoes were identical.

In 1817, the Duke of Wellington commissioned the boots that would become synonymous with his name. The rubberized version was introduced in the 1850s by the North British Rubber Company.

19th Century Innovations in Shoe Manufacturing

June 15, 1844: Charles Goodyear receives a patent for vulcanized rubber, a chemical process that uses heat to meld rubber to fabric or other components for a permanent bond.

1858: American Lyman Reed Blake earns a patent for the sewing machine that stitches the soles to the uppers.

January 24, 1871: Charles Goodyear, Jr patents the Goodyear Welt for sewing boots and shoes.

1883: Jan Ernst Matzeliger patents an automatic method for lasting shoes = mass production of affordable shoes.

January 24, 1899: Humphrey O'Sullivan patents the first rubber heel for shoes. Later, Elijah McCoy invents an improved rubber heel.

METALS

17. The Miner

Miners' lives in the 1800s were absurdly dangerous, largely in part because many technologies we now take for granted hadn't been invented yet. Even outside of the mines, life was uncertain. It was dangerous enough prospecting out West above ground, but the dangers increased hundredfold once you went down in the mines. Cave-ins were frequent. Poisoned, crushed, or frozen to death, being a miner, miller, or prospector could be deadly.

The day started early and ended late for miners and others working in the mines. Mining companies expected their workers to be down in the mine at 7:00 a.m. ready to go.

The Gold Rush in California began in 1849 and at first was a small, personal endeavor. Single prospectors or relatively unorganized groups of so-called 49ers simply panned for gold.

The silver bonanza started about ten years after the Gold Rush. There was Pikes Peak in Colorado, which yielded gold and silver in 1859; perhaps the most valuable discovery was the Comstock Lode in Nevada. Americans had almost no experience in processing silver. Many techniques were tried, typically with highly toxic chemicals.

18. The Smiths

Blacksmiths made tools, fences, and ornaments from iron. They were essential merchants and craftsmen in every American town. They made indispensable items such as horseshoes, pots, pans, and nails. Blacksmiths (sometimes called farriers) made numerous goods for farmers and horsemen.

The road to becoming a successful blacksmith was long and hard. Apprenticeships started at age 14 or 15 and could last up to seven years. At first, an apprentice would simply observe his master before helping with easy tasks.

Silversmiths were among the most numerous of craftsmen. Some silversmiths in America were forced to make their livings by importing silverware from England and selling it.

Silversmiths fashioned their objects from ingots, thick "bricks" of metal. Upon an anvil, the ingot would be hammered until it was thin. It was then placed over a stake to be shaped and smoothed.

Gunsmiths were considered extremely skilled craftsmen in the 1700s. Firearms were all constructed by hand. In this way, every gun was a one-of-a-kind possession; a broken gun could not be easily repaired. At the very least, the process was time consuming and expensive, as the gun had to be brought to a craftsman and repaired to order.

Guns and gunsmiths were critical to survival of early European American settlements, success in the Revolutionary War, the westward expansion, and triumph in the Industrial Revolution. Firearms manufacturers were also responsible for fundamental technological innovations, such as interchangeable parts and the American system of manufacturing.

Eli Whitney first made his name at the tender age of 27 with his invention of the cotton gin, patented in 1794.

From 1850, metalworking industries concentrated on technical improvements in manufacturing. With some initial assistance from Eli Whitney, Samuel Colt developed molds for forging the metal pieces of the revolver; hence, allowing for mass production.

****

****

TRANSPORTATION

19. The Teamster

Originally the term **teamster** referred to a person who drove a team, usually of oxen, horses, or mules, pulling a wagon. A teamster, AKA wagoner, waggoner, carter, looked after the horses under his control and drove them for whatever work was to be done, e.g., ploughing, reaping, harrowing, carting, etc. Otherwise, he drove a horse-drawn heavy four-wheeled wagon, carrying produce or manufactured goods to a market or railway station.

From the Revolutionary War at least through World War I, United States Army enlisted personnel responsible for transporting supplies by wagon and upkeep of animals for this purpose were called wagoners.

The role of a wagoner was to transport the supplies needed by the army. He was responsible for driving the wagon and maintaining it, feeding and caring for the mule team. It was an essential job, one that is too often overlooked when studying military history.

20. The Wheelwright

The wheelwright's craft is among the oldest in human history. In the nineteenth century, nearly every village had a wheelwright. They were important tradesman in every area. They made wheels for wagons, carriages, and riding chairs. Because early roads were rocky and rugged, wheels had to be made to handle the rough conditions. Wheelwrights also built or repaired carts, wheelbarrows, and wagons. They also made the wheels, and often the frames, for spinning wheels for home use.

Constructing such a wheel was considerably difficult and took the skills of metal working and carpentry. Wheelwrights cut, chiseled, fashioned, and shaped wheels from wood. The spokes and hubs were also made of wood. They used iron rims, often made by local blacksmiths, to fit around the exterior of the wheels.

A wide range of skills were used to make spoked wooden wheels. Tremendous forces acted upon wheels when in use. The wheelwright had to appreciate these forces fully.

It was necessary that the wheelwright worked with the village blacksmith. He would need to provide the blacksmith with the finished measurements, based upon the expected loading of the cart.

As metallurgy improved, iron strakes were replaced by a solid iron rim custom-made by the blacksmith. Rims were always made smaller than the wheel in circumference, expanded by heating in a fire then hammered and pulled on the wheel. It was released into the "ducking pond" of water. This shrank it onto the wood, closing the wooden joints.

RESOURCES

1. The Farmer

The Farmer https://www.historyforkids.net/an-agricultural-economy.html

History of Agriculture
https://en.wikipedia.org/wiki/History_of_agriculture_in_the_United_States

2. The Plowman

A Brief History of The Plough - https://www.ploughmen.co.uk/about-us/history-of-the-plough

Plowman - Surnames - https://www.genealogy.com/forum/surnames/topics/plowman/

The Phantom Plowman - A Spring Ghost Story from Pennsylvania - https://historybecauseitshere.weebly.com/the-phantom-plowman.html

3. The Orchardman

The Real Johnny Appleseed Brought Apples— and Booze—to the American Frontier https://www.smithsonianmag.com/arts-culture/real-johnny-appleseed-brought-applesand-booze-american-frontier-180953263/

A Curious Tale: The Apple in North America - By Tim Hensley | June 2, 2005 -- https://www.bbg.org/gardening/article/the_apple_in_north_america

Hard Cider: A Story of War, Immigration, and Prohibition - https://www.threeriversparks.org/blog/hard-cider-story-war-immigration-and-prohibition

4. The Fisherman

18th Century Fishing Techniques https://www.youtube.com/watch?v=OAP8ICY_3Lw

Ask Rufus: The Fish Trap - https://cdispatch.com/opinions/2018-12-08/ask-rufus-the-fish-trap/

Fishing Weir -
https://en.wikipedia.org/wiki/Fishing_weir

5. The Net Maker

The History of Net Making -
https://www.henrycowls.net/blog-en/the-history-of-net-making.html

6. The Sail Maker

Sailmaker -
https://en.wikipedia.org/wiki/Sailmaker

Sails and the Art of the Sailmaker -
https://www.philipkallan.com/single-post/2018/07/09/sails-and-the-vanishing-art-of-the-sailmaker

The Tradition of Making Sails Is a Specialized Skill -
https://www.thehour.com/sports/article/The-tradition-of-making-sails-is-a-specialized-8308872.php

7. The Miller

Gristmill -
https://en.wikipedia.org/wiki/Gristmill#Early_history

Sawmill -
https://en.wikipedia.org/wiki/Sawmill#Early_history

The French-Canadian Genealogist -
https://www.tfcg.ca/old-occupation-miller2*

8. The Printer

The History of Print from 1800 to 1849 -
https://www.prepressure.com/printing/history/180

0-
1849#:~:text=1800%20%E2%80%93%20Iron%20pres
ses,around%20200%20impressions%20per%20hour

9. The Mailman

13 Colonies Printer

https://mrnussbaum.com/printer-trade

A Brief History of the United States Postal Service - Winifred Gallagher - October 2020
https://www.smithsonianmag.com/smithsonian-institution/brief-history-united-states-postal-service-180975627/

The Many Ways Letters Were Carried in 18th- and Early 19th ... https://stamps.org›news›cat›postal-history›post

Mail Delivery

https://www.history.com/news/post-office-mail-delivery

10. The Telegrapher

Morse Code & the Telegraph -
https://www.history.com/topics/inventions/telegraph#:~:text=Developed%20in%20the%2018
30s%20and,a%20wire%20laid%20between%20stations

The Railroad Telegrapher by Jim Thompson -
https://thelibrary.org/lochist/periodicals/ozarkswatch/ow702h.htm

The Telegraph by David Hochfelder The
Telegraph - Essential Civil War Curriculum

The Telegraphers - https://chrisenss.com/the-telegraphers-3/

Telegraphist -
https://en.wikipedia.org/wiki/Telegraphist

11. The Brick Maker

13 Colonies Brickmaker -
https://mrnussbaum.com/brickmaker-trade
Brickmaking in the USA: A Brief History
Brickmaking History (brickcollecting.com)

12. The Carpenter

American historic carpentry -
https://en.wikipedia.org/wiki/American_historic_carpentry
Carpentry From Wikipedia, the free encyclopedia
- https://en.wikipedia.org/wiki/Carpentry
Carpentry in the 1800s -
https://carpenterslocal308.org/history#one
What did a carpenter do in the 1800s?
https://answerstoall.com/common-questions/what-did-a-carpenter-do-in-the-1800s/#What_did_a_carpenter_do_in_the_1800s

13. The Cooper

13 Colonies Cooper -
https://mrnussbaum.com/13-colonies-cooper
Craft Traditions – Cooperage
https://www.nh.gov/folklife/learning-center/traditions/cooperage.htm

14. The Mason – Brick and Stone

Difference Between a Mason and a Bricklayer?
https://www.avenueroadmasonry.com/2019/03/difference-mason-bricklayer/

Early American Masonry Materials ...- Harlei J. McKee, PAIA Copyright 1971 Harley J. McKee - extension://elhekieabhbkpmcefcoobjddigjcaad p/http://ip51.icomos.org/~fleblanc/documents/masonry/doc_early-american-masonry_McKee_1971.pdf

History of Brick Masonry - https://masonry-restoration.com/history-of-brick-masonry/

15. The Saddle Maker

13 Colonies Saddlemaker - https://mrnussbaum.com/saddlemaker-2

Old Ways Old Trades – The Saddle Maker https://www.outdoorrevival.com/instant-articles/old-ways-old-trades-the-saddle-maker.html?edg-c=1

16. The Cobbler

13 Colonies Cobbler - https://mrnussbaum.com/cobbler

The History of Shoes - Footwear from Ancient Times to the 20th Century https://www.thoughtco.com/history-of-shoes-1992405

17. The Miner

How Miners Lived, Dressed, and Died in the 1800s - https://www.heddels.com/2020/02/what-the-miners-actually-wore/

A Day in the Life of a Miner -- https://www.breckheritage.com/a-day-in-the-life-of-a-miner

18. The Smiths

13 Colonies Blacksmith

https://mrnussbaum.com/13-colonies-blacksmith

American Firearms and Their Makers: A Research Guide - https://guides.loc.gov/american-firearms

Firearms -

https://www.history.com/topics/inventions/firearms

Interchangeable Parts -

https://www.history.com/topics/inventions/interchangeable-parts

19. The Teamster

What Did a Wagoner Do? -

https://civilwartalk.com/threads/what-did-a-wagoner-do.24782/

What Is a Waggoner? -

https://www.rootschat.com/forum/index.php?topic=202986.0

20. The Wheelwright

13 Colonies Wheelwright -

https://mrnussbaum.com/13-colonies-wheelwright

Rural Life in Victorian England - Rural Life in Victorian England • FamilySearch

Wheelwright -

https://en.wikipedia.org/wiki/Wheelwright

www.ingramcontent.com/pod-product-compliance
Lightning Source LLC
Chambersburg PA
CBHW060922130726
48001CB00006B/2357